A guide to letter contracts

for very small projects, surveys and reports

Roland Phillips

Royal Institute of British Architects

© RIBA Enterprises Ltd, 2009

Published by RIBA Publishing, 15 Bonhill Street, London EC2P 2EA

ISBN 978 1 85946 314 7

Stock Code 68969

The right of Roland Phillips to be identified as the Author of this Work have been asserted in accordance with the Copyright, Design and Patents Act 1988.

All rights reserved. No part of this publication may be reproduced, stored in a retrieval system, or transmitted, in any form or by any means, electronic, mechanical, photocopying, recording or otherwise, without prior permission of the copyright owner.

British Library Cataloguing in Publications Data
A catalogue record for this book is available from the British Library.

Author: Roland Phillips
Publisher: Steven Cross
Commissioning Editor: Matthew Thompson
Designed and typeset by Philip Handley
Printed and bound by Windsor Print, Tonbridge, Kent, UK

While every effort has been made to ensure the accuracy and quality of information in this publication, the Publisher accepts no responsibility for the subsequent use of this information, for any errors or omissions that it may contain, or for any misunderstandings arising from it.

RIBA Publishing is part of RIBA Enterprises Ltd, www.ribaenterprises.com

Cover image © Jupiterimages

Foreword

During my years in small practice I found that a letter of appointment was more proportionate to the scale of very small commissions than the use of a more complex appointment document. Of course, no matter how scaled down a letter is, it must include certain basic elements as a minimum to meet the code requirements for setting out terms of appointment and scope of services in writing. For most work, one of the range of RIBA standard agreements is still the safest way to form a contract. However, for very small works, feasibility studies, short reports and so on, many clients find standard forms unnecessarily complex. In these circumstances, after carefully considering the nature and risks of the commission, the architect may, as I did, decide that letters of appointment are more appropriate.

This short guide provides architects with critically important information on the content and legal provisions, including obligations, calculation of fees and expenses, limits of liability and insurance, copyright, provisions for suspension and termination and dispute resolution, which even a simple letter of appointment must contain for the protection and benefit of both parties. It includes model letters and worked examples for use with consumer and business clients.

I feel sure that practices engaged in very small jobs will find this new guide an invaluable resource. It represents an important complementary alternative to the widely used RIBA Agreements and will, I am sure, become an essential reference for the architect in practice.

Ruth Reed, RIBA President Elect, June 2009

Contents

1 Letter contracts: Introduction — Page 7
   1.1 Definitions — 7
   1.2 RIBA Agreements for small projects — 7
   1.3 Choosing a Letter Contract — 7
   1.4 What should an architect's contract include? — 8
   1.5 The model Letter Contracts — 9

2 Watch-points — 11
   2.1 The consequences of a Letter Contract — 11
   2.2 Non-payment of fees — 11
   2.3 Copyright and assignment — 12
   2.4 Liability and insurance — 12
   2.5 Getting started — 13
   2.6 Ending the contract — 13

3 The model Letter Contracts — 15
   3.1 Model for a Business Client — 15
   3.2 Model for a Domestic Client — 21

4 Worked examples — 27
   4.1 Business works — 28
   4.2 Home works — 30
   4.3 A very small commission — 34
   4.4 Inspection and report — 36

Further reading — 37

1 Letter Contracts: Introduction

In deciding to use a Letter Contract, the parties should carefully consider whether they are compatible with the complexity of the project, the proposed procurement route and the risks to the parties.

If there is any doubt about the suitability of a Letter Contract (or an RIBA agreement) the architect should take legal advice.

1.1 Definitions

A Letter Contract may be defined as:
A contract in letter format – the 'Letter of Appointment' – which contains all of the principal terms and conditions within the body of the letter, to which might be attached any project-specific information such as a services schedule.

A Very Small Project may be defined as:
- for a **business client** as a non-notifiable project under the Construction (Design and Management) Regulations 2007, i.e. where construction work is not expected to last longer than 30 working days or involve more than 500 person-days;
- for a **domestic client** as a project where the cost of building work will not exceed, say, £40,000; or
- as a survey or other limited commission, for example, a feasibility study, building survey or accessibility audit.

1.2 RIBA Agreements for small projects

The conditions to the RIBA 'Concise Agreement' and 'Domestic Project Agreement' are expressed in simple terms and are used with a Letter of Appointment and an optional schedule 'Services for a Small Project'. The RIBA recommends these agreements for all small projects.

The first incorporates the statutory provisions which only apply to business clients or public authorities. The second takes account of the Unfair Terms in Consumer Contracts Regulations 1999.

1.3 Choosing a Letter Contract

Common sense says that when you are travelling you should take out adequate travel insurance: a new commission is the start of a journey for both client and architect, and the contract is the insurance policy.

Where the architect, after carefully considering the nature and risks of the commission, decides not to use an RIBA Agreement, a 'Letter of Appointment for a Very Small Project' may be appropriate.

But the Letter of Appointment should be reasonably balanced between architect and client, although it will omit or shorten many of the provisions included in RIBA Agreements.

Letter contracts should only be used where the architect is confident that the resulting contract will be fair to the client despite the inherent risks.

1 ▪ Letter Contracts: **Introduction**

1.4 What should an architect's contract include?

1.4.1 RIBA Code of Professional Conduct Guidance Note 4 says:
When proposing or confirming an appointment, a member should ensure that its terms and scope of works are clear and recorded in writing.

When contracting to supply architectural services, the terms of appointment should include:
- *a clear statement of the client's requirements*
- *a clear definition of the services required*
- *the obligation to perform the services with due skill and care*
- *the obligation to keep the client informed of progress*
- *the roles of other parties who will provide services to the project*
- *the name of any person(s) with authority to act on behalf of the client*
- *procedures for calculation and payment of fees and expenses*
- *any limitation of liability and insurance*
- *provisions for protection of copyright and confidential information*
- *provisions for suspension and determination*
- *provisions for dispute resolution*

1.4.2 The Architects Registration Board Architects Code is similar, but includes a requirement that architects inform the client that individual architects are required to be registered with the Architects Registration Board, are subject to its Code and to the disciplinary sanction of the Board in relation to complaints of unacceptable professional conduct or serious professional incompetence.

1.4.3 *Business clients*
A contract with a business client should be compatible with the requirements of:
- a 'construction contract' under the Housing Grants, Construction and Regeneration Act 1996 (HGCRA); and
- the client's duties under the Construction (Design and Management) Regulations 2007 (CDM).

Business clients include public authorities, charities, religious organisations and not-for-profit bodies.

1.4.4 *Domestic clients*
Where the client is a 'consumer' as defined under the Unfair Terms in Consumer Contracts Regulations 1999 (UTCCR), that is 'a natural person acting for purposes outside his trade, business or profession, i.e. who will sign in his/her own name, i.e. not as a limited company or other legal entity', it is essential to read through the terms of the agreement with the client and agree each term separately.

The Letter of Appointment may be a convenient way of recording the substance of the negotiations and should minimise the risk that any of the terms may subsequently be considered to be unfair. It is not unheard of for a consumer to claim subsequently that they did not understand the implications of a term. Note that UTCC Regulation 8(1) says that, 'An unfair term in a contract concluded with a consumer by a seller or supplier shall not be binding on the consumer.'

If the client is a married couple or joint residential occupiers, all the client parties are consumers, but the client should identify one of their number as their representative with full authority to act on behalf of the parties and to sign the agreement.

Work to the client's home or to a second home will be exempt from:
- the provisions of the Housing Grants, Construction and Regeneration Act 1996 (HGCR) as a 'residential occupier'
- the Construction (Design and Management) Regulations 2007
- the Late Payment of Commercial Debts (Interest) Regulations 2002.

But if the client's second home is to be let at any time as a holiday rental or to other tenants the client will be a business client and the exemptions will not apply.

A company may also be a 'consumer' subject to Unfair Contract Terms Act 1977 (but not subject to UTCCR) if the transaction is *only incidental to its business activity and which is not of a kind that it makes with any degree of regularity*. It may be a wise precaution and courteous to treat such consumers as though the UTCCR did apply. But a 'consumer' who is not a 'residential occupier' will **not** be exempt from HCCRA or exempt from the CDM Regulations if not a 'domestic client' as defined in the CDM Regulations.

1.5 The model Letter Contracts

A Letter Contract will comprise the Letter of Appointment and any appendices recording relevant project specific information e.g. the schedule 'Services for a Small Project'. No separate conditions are required.

The models for 'Very Small Projects' are:
- carefully devised to simplify the presentation
- expressed in plain, intelligible language
- derived from the provisions of the RIBA Concise and Domestic Project Agreements
- inclusive of provisions, some optional, that can be selected, modified or deleted by the architect to meet project-specific requirements and/or the perceived risks.

There are two model contracts, one to a business client and the other to a domestic client. The RIBA schedule 'Services for a Small Project' may be suitable for use with such Very Small Projects.

The worked examples (Section 4) indicate how the architect can create contracts based on the models for a wide range of commissions.

The model Letter of Appointment is available in RTF format and can be downloaded free of charge from www.ribabookshops.com/lettercontracts.

The schedule 'Services for a Small Project' is available in RTF format and can be downloaded from www.ribabookshops.com/agreements.

2 Watchpoints

2.1 The consequences of a Letter Contract

Simplification entails omitting or shortening provisions and related procedures included in RIBA Agreements.

Some optional provisions are included in the models in order to:
- reduce the risk of non-payment of fees
- cover issues arising from the copyright licence
- limit liability to other persons or arising from the default of others.

OR [Because the client must comply with the law, it is not essential to define the obligations that arise from compliance with statutory requirements, except where choices have to be made, e.g. for particular dispute resolution procedures.]

If the architect considers that such simplified provisions substantially increase the risks of a specific commission, it is probable that either the RIBA 'Concise Agreement' or the 'Domestic Project Agreement' will be more appropriate.

A short contract does not diminish the normal standards of performance required of an architect. Indeed, a short contract might, paradoxically, increase the architect's obligations in some instances, because the law will usually imply certain minimum standards which may be higher than those set by a longer, tighter contract (e.g. provisions limiting the liability of the architect).

Separate Conditions
The models include the issues that need to be considered when the architect drafts a project-specific letter. Many architects produce their own separate one-page Conditions used in conjunction with a letter, sometimes for projects costing up to as much as £250,000 or more. Such Conditions should:
- be expressed in plain intelligible language, in a type size to aid comprehension, and large enough to be read comfortably by readers whose vision is impaired
- include all the essential terms without duplicating matters covered by the letter
- not conflict with statutory requirements.

2.2 Non-payment of fees

Numbered note 8 to each of the model letters models explains the options which may be included in the letters to provide for non-payment of 'sums properly due'.

Suspension of the copyright licence (see numbered note 6), in the event of non-payment, is a powerful weapon, particularly if the client needs the drawings etc to raise funds or for construction.

Business clients are subject to both the Late Payment of Commercial Debts (Interest) Act 1988 and the requirement to issue a withholding notice if HGCRA applies. If the client fails to issue a notice and sets off any sums due, the architect has the right to suspend performance of all obligations.

There are no similar statutes applicable to consumer clients. However, in the absence of express terms both parties will have rights at law to refer a payment dispute to the courts (unless an arbitration clause is included in the contract) or to terminate the commission and claim damages (if the situation is serious enough) or to implement debt recovery procedures.

See also *Good Practice Guide: Fee Management* (RIBA Publishing, 2009).

2 ■ Letter Contracts: **Watchpoints**

2.3 Copyright and assignment

RIBA Agreements include provisions to protect the architect's copyright and terms for the licence to copy and use the information produced by the architect subject to payment of sums properly due.

The Letter Contract should also do so. If it is silent about copyright, a subsequent purchaser of the property is likely to have an implied licence to use the copyright material for all purposes connected with the erection of a building on the property in substantial accordance with the copyright material.

For this reason, it is important for the architect to consider the risks associated with the use of that copyright material and to require the architect's prior consent to any assignment.

However, if a report or design is requested by a client who intends to sell, lease or let the property, ensure that the amount of liability (see Section 2.4) is specified in the letter, and consider whether the optional reference providing for consent before any copyright material may be used by *any future purchaser, leaseholder or tenant of your property* is necessary. This will afford the architect the opportunity to negotiate appropriate limitations on liability with any interested third party.

To deter the licensee from arranging for another person to amend any copyright material in a way that would have an adverse effect on the architect's reputation, the optional assertion of the architect's moral rights under the Copyright, Designs and Patents Act 1988 in the model gives the architect the right to be identified as the author of the work and to object to derogatory treatment of that work.

2.4 Liability and insurance

The period of liability is *'six years from completion of the Services'*. RIBA Agreements also say '*or, if earlier, after practical completion of the construction of the Project or such earlier date as prescribed by law*'. That *'earlier date'* may apply to a breach of contract, for instance for a design defect, where the statutory period runs from the date of the breach, which is likely to be earlier than the contractual time limit.

Architects must maintain insurance for not less than the amount required by the Architects Registration Board and include cover for legal defence costs, but it is not essential to make this a term of the contract (although to do so may be seen as 'added value' by the client).

However, the limitation in the amount of liability should always be stated and, where there is any risk of claims arising from asbestos or pollution, any limits that apply in the aggregate in any year of insurance should also be stated.

In the models, liability to the client may be limited by way of a sum per occurrence to match the usual term for professional indemnity insurance. However, the models do not include a net contribution provision because it seems unlikely that such a provision would pass the reasonable test under the Unfair Contract Terms Act 1977 for a small project. For this reason it may be appropriate to agree an aggregate cap on liability to cover all claims, i.e. not just individual claims.

It may seem overkill for a Very Small Project or a report, but consider the risks if, for instance, a report that had been relied on by a purchaser overlooked some important fact, or a defect in a design caused a catastrophic collapse of a building resulting in damage to other property, or the builder became insolvent.

The amount of cover may be less than that carried by the architect's practice. It may be necessary to discuss the project with the insurers/broker about the provisions of the models and/or if the use of sub-consultants is proposed.

2.5 Getting started

It is a requirement of the RIBA, the ARB and insurers that at the outset of any project an agreement is made in writing. If it is not possible to finalise an agreement, perhaps because the scope of the brief, the services or the time and cost parameters need significant development, write to the client explaining the basis on which it is proposed to proceed, enclosing a draft of the Letter Contract, the anticipated basis for fees and ask for instructions.

To minimise the risk of misunderstanding, it is also important to consider whether all the matters discussed, recorded or not, are covered by the contract when it is signed.

For a contract to come into being, a clear agreement must be reached through the making of an offer and acceptance of that offer. It would be reasonable to assume that a contract has come into being if, after receipt of an offer, the client acts in accordance with it, thereby indicating acceptance of the offer.

If no response is received, however, it would be prudent for the architect to seek confirmation from the client that the offer is acceptable before proceeding with the services. If the response is: 'Please get on with the services, and we can negotiate', the effect would be uncertain and unsatisfactory.

Of course, the best idea is to visit the client, agree the terms and get them signed there and then. However, a contributor on the RIBAnet discussion forum described his practice's approach:

> I am sure that if I insisted that small businesses or domestic clients signed the agreement, I would lose 80% of my work. I could chase and hassle them to sign, but that risks alienating them and takes additional non-fee-earning time. There also appears to be a perception amongst small businesses that getting things in writing costs time and money, cutting into profits, and some clients do not see a signed agreement as 'professional' but a way of the service provider getting out of its responsibilities.
>
> If there is no response, in order to establish the relationship, I confirm the date of the survey in writing and add a reference to 'payment in accordance with our appointment dated …' in fee accounts.

It is a pity if such a pragmatic approach is necessary, but remember that it is prudent for the architect to deliver the specific and implied obligations in the unsigned contract so as to preserve their position in the event of there being a subsequent dispute over the terms of the contract.

2.6 Ending the contract

The models include provisions allowing the client or the architect to suspend or end performance of the contract by giving at least seven days' written notice and stating the reason for doing so.

There is specific provision for suspension by the architect for non-payment of fees (see Section 2.2 above).

However, the right to terminate the contract should only be exercised with extreme caution. If the situation cannot be resolved by negotiation, legal advice should be obtained about how to proceed.

3 The model Letter Contracts

3.1 Letter Contracts: Model for a Business Client

> *This model Letter of Appointment can be downloaded free of charge from www.ribabookshops.com/lettercontracts.*
>
> *The schedule 'Services for a Small Project' can be downloaded from www.ribabookshops.com/agreements.*

Numbered notes

The contract with a business client (see Section 1.4.3) will comprise the letter containing all the terms and conditions with any appendices necessary to record relevant project specific information, e.g. the schedule 'Services for a Small Project'.

The letter is signed as a simple contract under the law of England and Wales. If the law of Scotland is applicable, some modifications may be necessary.

The numbered notes and the model text identify some optional provisions that may be selected by the architect to meet project-specific requirements and/or risks, and some that may be omitted without reducing the legal obligations of either party, for instance:
- the standard of *reasonable skill and care*, which will be implied in the contract by law
- defining the obligations that arise from compliance with statutory requirements because the client must comply with the law – a brief summary of applicable legislation is given in *A client's guide to engaging an architect* (RIBA Publishing, 2009).

After careful consideration of project specific requirements, the architect should consider, select, modify or delete the provisions of the model text to take account of such requirements.

If the model text is not used, be careful that other wording does not modify or conflict with other provisions of the contract. The essential requirement is that all the necessary information is recorded in the letter and/or in an appendix.

1 For purposes of identification, insert accurate names and addresses of the parties to the agreement.

2 The letter should be formal – Dear [Sir] [Madam]. Yours faithfully... for and on behalf of [the practice]. Ensure that the title and the location of the project are accurately stated.

3 The scope of the work should include an initial statement or note of the client's requirements on which the services and fees will be based.

If it is not available at the date of the letter, the architect will need to ascertain any necessary phasing requirements, environmental or design quality standards, and any landlord or similar approvals required and information about the site. Under CDM 2007 Regulation 10, a business client (whether or not the project is 'notifiable') is required to provide relevant information likely to be needed by designers, contractors or others to plan and manage their work.

3 ■ Letter Contracts: **The model Letter Contracts**

This information may need to include operational/organisational matters, the client's working methods and safety policies, any health and safety file or other information about or affecting the site or the construction work.

4 If the RIBA schedule 'Services for a Small Project' is used, tick the boxes for the services required or enter 'T' for time-charged services or 'LS' for lump sums. If different or extra services are needed for the particular project, these can be described and identified as 'other services' where indicated. An on-line supplement to the schedule is available for a historic building or conservation project.

Alternatively, describe the services required in the letter or devise a project-specific schedule, perhaps using the editable on-line rtf version of the RIBA schedule.

5 It is wise to ensure that the client is clear about the extent of the architect's appointment, and understands their role in relation to the appointment of other consultants, payment of fees, etc.

6 The model includes options to assert the moral right, which may help to avoid 'derogatory treatment' of the work and also to draw the attention to the contractual requirement for the architect's consent to assign the contract or the licence to another party.

The copyright licence is subject to payment of fees (see item 8 below).

7 There is no standard or recommended basis for defining the fee, which is usually a matter for negotiation. Where appropriate, the fee may be a percentage of the building cost or a lump sum (see Section 1.5). In cases where the scope of the work is harder to predict, or for services such as surveys or party wall advice, the quotation will often consist of an hourly or daily rate, together with an estimate of the time required.

Indication of the fee for each stage, or group of stages, will prove beneficial if changes are made subsequently to the cost or the programme. Indicating the number of site visits during construction will provide an opportunity to claim for extra visits if all does not go according to plan.

Carefully list the expenses to be reimbursed; by implication this therefore defines those not covered. Where the net cost option applies, state the rates for copies of documents and the mileage rate for travel by car.

See also *Good Practice Guide: Fee management* (RIBA Publishing, 2009).

8 In the event of non-payment of fees, the architect may
- suspend use of the copyright licence (see item 6 above)
- invoke the Late Payment of Commercial Debts (Interest) Act 1988 which gives a statutory right to interest at 8% over the Bank of England base rate on late payments and recovery costs
- suspend performance of all obligations if the client fails to issue a withholding notice as required by HGCRA. This may be an effective remedy whilst the pre-construction, construction and post-completion stages are in progress. It will be less effective if it is the final payment(s) that are withheld. If the notice is issued, the architect may refer the issue to the dispute resolution procedures (see also Section 2.2).

However it is not necessary to include any of the options in the letter because the provisions of the relevant statutes will automatically apply to a business client, and use of the copyright licence is subject to payment of fees etc.

9 See Section 2.4 for notes on liability and insurance.

10 The model provides for resolving disputes by negotiation or mediation, adjudication or legal proceedings, but it does not mention arbitration which seems an unlikely choice for Very Small Projects. The adjudication procedures in the Scheme for

Construction Contracts regulations automatically apply under the HGCR Act unless an alternative scheme is selected. It is not essential to specify the adjudicator nominating body in the contract.

It should be explained to the client that a JCT or similar published building contract may include different arrangements for dispute resolution.

Adjudicator nominating bodies for use if required include:

Royal Institute of British Architects
Construction Industry Council
Royal Incorporation of Architects in Scotland
Royal Institution of Chartered Surveyors
Technology and Construction Solicitors' Association.

11 Both parties execute the contract as a simple contract by signing both copies of the Letter where indicated. It is not necessary to witness signatures to a simple contract unless confirmation of identity is required. Any attachments, e.g. the services schedule but not guidance notes, should be in duplicate and initialled by both parties.

3 Letter Contracts: **The model Letter Contracts**

3.1 Letter Contracts: Model for a Business Client

> *This model Letter of Appointment can be downloaded free of charge from www.ribabookshops.com/lettercontracts.*
>
> *The schedule 'Services for a Small Project' can be downloaded from www.ribabookshops.com/agreements.*

Refer to the numbered notes, adapting the model text as appropriate. (Items in square brackets are optional or alternatives.) On completion, delete the numbered note references in the models.

1   From architect – <full business name and address>

  To client – <full business name and address>

  [For the attention of …]

2   Dear [Sir] [Madam]

  [Project] [at]:

3   Thank you for inviting me/us to act as architect for this project [as described in the attached notes of our meeting on <date>] [as described in your letter of <date>] [which are to be based on the attached sketch proposal developed at our meeting on <date>].

  You told me/us that your target cost for the building work is £<amount> to which must be added fees and any VAT. You also said that you would like building works to [commence on] [be complete by] <date>.

The services

4   [You have asked me/us to <describe the professional services required>] [My/Our services are described in the attached schedule 'Services for a Small Project' in the before-construction stages] [and in the subsequent construction stages.] [You told me/us that you will manage the construction stages including obtaining tenders and overseeing the building work.]

  [In providing the services I/we will exercise reasonable skill and care, act as your representative and advise you on any issues affecting the time, cost or quality of your project. I/We will not make any material changes to the services or the agreed design except in an emergency [nor subcontract any of the Services] without your consent.]

  [I/We will also advise you on compliance with statutory legislation [and enclose for your information a copy of [*A client's guide to engaging an architect*] and [*A client's guide to health and safety on a construction project* which outlines your duties under the Construction (Design and Management) Regulations 2007 (CDM), which I/we hope you will find helpful]]].

  [At this stage it would not appear that it will be necessary to notify your project to the Health and Safety Executive under the CDM Regulations]. [If the project does become notifiable to the HSE, you will be required to appoint a CDM Coordinator (and, in due course, a principal contractor) in accordance with the Regulations.] [I [attach] [confirm sending to you on <date>] an information pack about our competence in relation to these Regulations.]

[When the extent of any work affecting the common wall with the adjoining property is determined, I/we can discuss the application of the Party Wall Act. Please note that it may be necessary to appoint a party wall surveyor if your neighbour objects to the work.]

5   [At this time, I/we do not believe that it will be necessary for you to seek advice from any other consultants.] [I/We have informed you that I/we will require the services of [a structural engineer] [quantity surveyor]. I/we will write separately about their appointment and the fees entailed.] [As agreed with you, I/we will engage <name> a firm of [structural engineers] [quantity surveyors] to advise me/us. I/we shall be responsible to you for their services, the costs of which are included in my/our fee.] If it becomes necessary to vary the services or to appoint other consultants, I/we will let you know and we can discuss how to proceed.

6   I/We own the copyright in the drawings and documents that I/we produce for your project [and I/we generally assert my/our moral rights to be identified as author of that work under the Copyright, Designs and Patents Act 1988] but subject to payment of fees and/or other amounts properly due, you may copy and use those drawings and documents for purposes related to your project only. [Your right to copy and use does not extend to any future purchaser, leaseholder or tenant of your property without my/our prior agreement.]

Fees and expenses

7   My/Our fee in the before-construction stages will be [<value>% of the pre-tender estimated cost of the building work] [a lump sum of £<amount>].

[For the construction stages, my/our fee will be [<value>% of the final cost of the building work excluding VAT, fees and any additional costs associated with claims made by or against the builder] [a lump sum of £<amount>], [this includes for [<number>] visits to the site in connection with my/our duties during construction] [charged on a time basis at £<amount> per hour]].

For [<describe service> identified by 'LS' in the schedule] the fee will be a [lump sum of £<amount>].

Extra services [and any services identified by 'T' in the schedule] will be charged at £<amount> per hour.

[My/Our fee includes my/our expenses.] [In addition to the fee[s], the cost of [copying or purchase of drawings and documents and travel] will be charged [plus a handling charge of <value>%] [by the addition of <value>% to] [each account] [the total fee]].

[Travel by car will be charged at <number>p per mile. Other expenses will be charged at net cost [plus <value>%]. I/We will ask you to send me/us a cheque for the fees payable to the local authority before making planning or Building Regulations applications].

I/We will issue an account [each month] [on completion of each work stage] for the fees and expenses due [plus VAT] and any disbursements less any amounts previously paid, and stating the basis of calculation of the amounts due. [VAT is not chargeable on my/our accounts as I am/we are not registered, but if this changes I/we will let you know.]

8   [Please note that if payment of any sums properly due is not made within 14 days, the Late Payment of Commercial Debts (Interest) Act 1988 will apply] [simple interest at 8% over the Bank of England base rate together with reasonable debt recovery costs will be payable] [and I/we may give at least seven days' written notice of my/our intention to suspend use of the copyright licence.]

3 ▪ Letter Contracts: **The model Letter Contracts**

Liability and insurance

9 My/Our liability to you will expire after six years from completion of the services [or, if earlier, after practical completion of the construction of the project or such earlier date as prescribed by law].

I/We agreed that my/our maximum liability to you for loss or damage will be limited to £<amount> in respect of each and every claim or series of claims arising out of the same originating cause, [within an overall cap of £<amount> for all claims] [except for claims arising out of:
- pollution and contamination, where the annual aggregate limit is £<amount>
- asbestos, where the limit for any one claim and in the aggregate of all claims is £<amount>]

[I/We shall maintain until the expiry of the liability period professional indemnity insurance cover for [that amount] [those amounts]].

[I/We should be pleased to provide documentary evidence of the insurance, if required.]

Disputes

10 I/We aim to provide a professional standard of service, but if at any time you are not satisfied, please bring the issue to my/our attention as soon as possible and we can discuss how to resolve the issue. [I/We hope that we will be able to settle the matter by negotiation or mediation. Alternatively, either of us can start court proceedings to settle the dispute at any time. But nothing shall prevent either of us from referring any dispute to adjudication at any time under the Scheme for Construction Contracts (England and Wales[1]) Regulations 1998. [Should we need help in choosing an adjudicator, the nominator will be <name of selected body>]].

Please note that individual architects are required to be registered with the Architects Registration Board, are subject to its Code and the disciplinary sanction of the Architects Registration Board in relation to complaints of unacceptable professional conduct or serious professional incompetence.

Signing the contract

11 If you agree with the contents of this letter, please sign both copies and initial, where indicated, both copies of the services schedule, [and <other specified attachments>[2]] and return one copy of the documents to me/us. I/We will then be in a position to start work.

I am/We are looking forward to working with you on this project.

Yours faithfully

for and on behalf of <practice name>

___

I/We confirm that [I/we have read and understood the terms set out in this letter and attachments and that] <practice name> are to proceed with the services as described.

Signed:_____   Date:_____

for and on behalf of <the client>

---

[1] Or Scotland or Northern Ireland   [2] Not including separate guidance

3.2 Letter contracts: Model for a Domestic Client

> *This model Letter of Appointment can be downloaded free of charge from www.ribabookshops.com/lettercontracts.*
>
> *The schedule 'Services for a Small Project' can be downloaded from www.ribabookshops.com/agreements.*

Domestic clients (see Section 1.4.4)

There have been a number of legal judgements against architects and surveyors who have failed to comply with the Unfair Terms in Consumer Contracts Regulations 1999 [UTCCR]. In particular, it is advisable to keep a close eye on Regulation 5(1) and the 'grey terms' (as one judge referred to them) set out in Schedule 2 to the UTCCR, as well as the 'reasonableness test' required by the Unfair Contract Terms Act 1977 (UCTA).

The consumer client must be given assistance to understand the obligations and the procedural options available. Adequate time must be given to the client to study the proposed agreement, to seek more information, to discover the meaning of particular provisions or to seek independent advice.

The architect should make a note of the negotiations, in particular drawing attention to those terms relating to payment, liability and dispute resolution and any amendments that are appropriate. Copy the note to the client as a record, so that it can be demonstrated that the negotiations were carried out in good faith, and that the reasons and consequences were clearly explained.

Numbered notes

The contract will comprise the letter containing all the terms and conditions with any appendices necessary to record relevant project-specific information, e.g. the schedule 'Services for a Small Project'.

The letter is signed as a simple contract under the law of England and Wales and Northern Ireland. If the law of Scotland is applicable, some modifications may be necessary.

The numbered notes and the model text identify some optional provisions that may be selected by the architect to meet project-specific requirements and/or risks, and some that may be omitted without reducing the legal obligations of either party, for instance:
- the standard of *reasonable skill and care*, which will be implied in the contract by law
- defining the obligations that arise from compliance with statutory requirements because the client must comply with the law. A brief summary of applicable legislation is given in *A client's guide to engaging an architect* (RIBA Publishing, 2009).

After careful consideration of project-specific requirements, the architect should consider, select, modify or delete the provisions of the model text to meet any perceived risks.

If the model text is not used, be careful that other wording does not modify or conflict with other provisions of the contract. The essential requirement is that all the necessary information is recorded in the letter and/or in an appendix.

3 ■ Letter Contracts: **The model Letter Contracts**

The numbered notes and the model text also include some provisions for dealing with terms that must be drawn to the client's attention to comply with the letter and spirit of the UTCCR.

1 For purposes of identification, insert accurate names and addresses of the parties to the contract.

2 The letter should be formal – Dear Mr and Mrs … Yours [faithfully] [sincerely] … for and on behalf of [the practice] – and avoid social or other comment that might subsequently cause conflict with what is intended to be a legal agreement. Ensure that the title and location of the project are accurately stated.

3 The scope of the work should include an initial statement or note of the client's requirements on which the services and fees will be based.

If it is not available at the date of the letter, the architect will need to ascertain any necessary phasing requirements, environmental or design quality standards, and any landlord or similar approvals required, and information about the site.

4 If the RIBA schedule 'Services for a Small Project' is used, tick the boxes for the services required or enter 'T' for time charged services or 'LS' for lump sums. If different or extra services are needed for the particular project, these can be described and identified as 'Other services' where indicated. An on-line supplement to the schedule is available for a historic building or conservation project.

Alternatively, describe the services required in the letter or devise a project-specific schedule, perhaps using the editable on-line rtf version of the RIBA schedule. Identify a new schedule with an appropriate reference.

Section 12.12 of the *Architect's handbook of practice management*, 7th edition (RIBA Enterprises, 2001) gives some useful advice about the risks associated with house inspections for the owner or a building society, etc.

5 It is wise to ensure that the client is clear about the extent of the appointment and understands his/her role in relation to the appointment of other consultants, payment of fees, etc.

6 The model includes options to assert the moral right, which may help to avoid 'derogatory treatment' of the work and to draw the attention of the client to the legal requirement for the architect's consent to transfer the contract or the licence to another party.

The copyright licence is subject to payment of fees (see item 8 below).

7 There is no standard or recommended basis for the calculation of the fee, which is usually a matter for negotiation. Where appropriate, the fee may be a percentage of the building cost or a lump sum (see Section 1.5). In cases where the scope of their work is harder to predict, or for services such as surveys or party wall advice, the quote will often consist of an hourly or daily rate together with an estimate of the time required.

Indication of the fee for each stage, or group of stages, will prove beneficial if changes are made subsequently to the cost or the programme. Indicating the number of site visits during construction will provide an opportunity to claim for extra visits if all does not go according to plan.

Carefully list the expenses to be reimbursed; by implication this therefore defines those not covered. Where the net cost option applies, state the rates for copies of documents and the mileage rate for travel by car.

8 To deal with non-payment of any sums properly due, the letter may include an enforceable contractual arrangement for interest at 8% over the Bank of England base rate, together with reasonable recovery costs.

The important words are 'sums properly due', if the architect agrees, or a tribunal finds, that the particular sums are not due, neither the related interest nor the costs will be payable (see also Section 2.2).

The copyright licence is also subject to the payment of fees and may be suspended for non-payment.

The Late Payment of Commercial Debts Regulations 2002 do not apply to consumer clients.

9 Note that UTTCR Schedule 2 item 1(b) states 'inappropriately excluding or limiting the legal rights of the consumer' may be regarded as unfair, and UCTA requires that any limitations of liability must be 'reasonable'.

Therefore, the limit should be agreed, taking into account the fee and potential risks involved, which might include, for instance, the risk of collateral damage if structural alterations are involved, to meet the objective of 'reasonableness' (see also Section 2.4).

10 The model provides for resolving disputes by negotiation, mediation, adjudication or legal proceedings. A consumer has the right to refer any dispute to the courts. Any other options must be negotiated. For instance, the consumer could choose arbitration, perhaps to keep the matter private, by incorporating appropriate provisions, although this seems an unlikely choice for Very Small Projects.

The consumer client may see the potential benefits of choosing contractual (non-statutory) adjudication. The RIBA Consumer Contracts Adjudication scheme provides for a maximum fee which would provide about 10 hours for the appointed adjudicator to deal with a dispute. If agreed, send the client a copy of the guide to the scheme, which is available from:

Royal Institute of British Architects
Disputes Resolution Office
66 Portland Place
London W1B 1AD.

T: 020 7307 3649
F: 020 7307 3793
E: adjudication@inst.riba.org

It should be explained to the client that a JCT, or similar published building contract, may include different arrangements for dispute resolution.

The model also includes an optional provision allowing the architect to suspend performance of all obligations and, if the terms of the licence allow, use of the copyright licence in the event of non-payment of fees, as an alternative to using the dispute resolution procedures. This may be an effective remedy whilst the pre-construction, construction or post-completion stages are in progress. It will be less effective if it is the final payment(s) that are withheld.

11 Both parties execute the contract as a simple contract by signing both copies of the letter where indicated. It is not necessary to witness signatures to a simple contract unless confirmation of identity is required. Any attachments, e.g. the services schedule but not guidance notes, should be in duplicate and initialled by both parties.

3 ■ Letter Contracts: **The model Letter Contracts**

3.2 Letter contracts: Model for a Domestic Client

> *This model Letter of Appointment can be downloaded free of charge from www.ribabookshops.com/lettercontracts.*
>
> *The schedule 'Services for a Small Project' can be downloaded from www.ribabookshops.com/agreements.*

Refer to the numbered notes, adapting the model text as appropriate. (Items in square brackets are optional or alternatives.) On completion delete the numbered note references in the models.

1 From Architect – <full business name and address>

To Client – <full business name and address>

[For the attention of …]

2 Dear [Mr] [and Mrs] [Sir] [Madam]

[Project] [at]:

3 Thank you for inviting me/us to act as architect for this project [as described in the attached notes of our meeting on <date>] [as described in your letter of <date>] [which are to be based on the attached sketch proposal developed at our meeting on <date>].

You told me/us that your target cost for the building work is £<amount> to which must be added fees and any VAT. You also said that you would like building works to [commence on] [be complete by] <date>.

The services

4 [You have asked me/us to <describe the professional services required>] [My/Our Services are described in the attached schedule 'Services for a Small Project' in the before-construction stages] [and in the subsequent construction stages.] [You told me/us that you will manage the construction stages including obtaining tenders and overseeing the building work.]

I/We will also advise you on compliance with statutory legislation [and enclose for your information a copy of [*Working with an architect for your home*] which I/we hope you will find helpful].

[In providing the Services I/we will exercise reasonable skill and care, act as your representative and advise you on any issues affecting the time, cost or quality of your project. I/We will not make any material changes to the Services or the agreed design except in an emergency [nor subcontract any of the Services] without your consent.]

[When the extent of any work affecting the common wall with the adjoining property is determined, we can discuss the application of the Party Wall Act. Please note that it may be necessary to appoint a party wall surveyor if your neighbour objects to the work.]

5 [At this time I/we do not believe that it will be necessary for you to seek advice from any other consultants.] [I/We have informed you that I/we will require the services of [a structural engineer] [quantity surveyor]. I/We will write separately about their appointment and the fees entailed.] [As agreed with you I/we will engage <name> a firm of [structural engineers] [quantity surveyors] to advise me/us. I/We shall be responsible to you for their services, the costs of which are included in my/our fee.]

If it becomes necessary to vary the services or to appoint other consultants, I/we will let you know and we can discuss how to proceed.

6 I/We own the copyright in the drawings and documents that I/we produce for your project [and I/we generally assert my/our moral rights to be identified as author of that work under the Copyright, Designs and Patents Act 1988] but, subject to payment and/or other amounts properly due, you may copy and use those drawings and documents for purposes related to your project only. [Your right to copy and use does not extend to any future purchaser, leaseholder or tenant of your property without my/our prior agreement.]

Fees and expenses

7 My/Our fee in the before-construction stages will be [<value>% of the pre-tender estimated cost of the building work excluding VAT and fees] [a lump sum of £<amount>].

[For the construction stages my/our fee will be [<value>% of the final cost of the building work excluding VAT, fees and any additional costs associated with claims made by or against the builder] [a lump sum of £<amount>], [this includes for [<number>] visits to the site in connection with my/our duties during construction] [charged on a time basis at £<amount> per hour]].

For [<describe service> identified by 'LS' in the schedule] the fee will be a [lump sum of £<amount>].

Extra services [and any services identified by 'T' in the schedule] will be charged at £<amount> per hour.

[My/Our fee includes my/our expenses.] [In addition to the fee[s], the cost of [copying or purchase of drawings and documents and travel] will be charged [plus a handling charge of <value>%] [by the addition of <value>% to] [each account] [the total fee]].

[Travel by car will be charged at <number>p per mile. Other expenses will be charged at net cost [plus <value>%]. I/We will ask you to send me/us a cheque for the fees payable to the local authority before making planning or Building Regulations applications].

I/We will submit an account for the fees and any expenses due [plus VAT] and any disbursements [each month] [on completion of each work stage]. [Monthly accounts will be based on the estimated percentage of completion.] Payment is to be made within 14 days. [VAT is not chargeable on my/our accounts as I am/we are not registered, but if this changes I/we will let you know.]

8 [Please note that if payment of any sums properly due is not made within 14 days, simple interest at 8% over the Bank of England base rate [together with reasonable debt recovery costs] will be payable [and I/we may suspend performance of all obligations and use of the copyright licence by giving at least 7 days' written notice]].

Liability and insurance

9 My/Our liability to you will expire after six years from completion of the Services [or, if earlier, after practical completion of the construction of the Project or such earlier date as prescribed by law].

We agreed that my/our maximum liability to you for loss or damage will be limited to £<amount> in respect of each and every claim or series of claims arising out of the same originating cause, [within an overall cap of £<amount> for all claims] [except

for claims arising out of:
- pollution and contamination, where the annual aggregate limit is £<amount>
- asbestos, where the limit for any one claim and in the aggregate of all claims is £<amount>]

[I/We shall maintain until the expiry of the liability period professional indemnity insurance cover for [that amount] [those amounts]].

[I/We should be pleased to provide documentary evidence of the insurance, if required.]

Disputes

10 I/We aim to provide a professional standard of service, but if at any time you are not satisfied, please bring the issue to my/our attention as soon as possible and we can discuss how to resolve the issue. [I/We hope that we will be able to settle the matter by negotiation or mediation. Alternatively, either of us can start court proceedings to settle the dispute at any time.] [Or, you have agreed that either of us can have the dispute decided within 21 days by an adjudicator appointed under the RIBA Consumer Adjudication scheme [for which I/we attach a guide]].

Please note that individual architects are required to be registered with the Architects Registration Board, are subject to its Code and the disciplinary sanction of the Architects Registration Board in relation to complaints of unacceptable professional conduct or serious professional incompetence.

Signing the contract

11 If you agree with the contents of this letter, please sign both copies, and initial, where indicated both copies of the services schedule, [and <other specified attachments>[1]] and return one copy of the documents to me/us. I/We will then be in a position to start work.

I/We are looking forward to working with you on this project.

Yours faithfully

for and on behalf of <practice name>

_____

I/We confirm that [I/we have read and understood the terms set out in this letter and attachments and that] <practice name> are to proceed with the services as described.

Signed:_____ Date:_____

for and on behalf of <the client>

---

[1] Not including separate guidance.

4 Worked examples

The worked examples demonstrate how the model text can be used as a basis for project-specific commissions. They also demonstrate that the format of downloaded rtf documents can be modified with different fonts, style etc to suit the preferences of the user.

4.1 Business works

In this example, the architect considered that the client understood the process and the risks. As the appointment was for all stages, the architect's letter is very close to the model text. The architect considered that it was appropriate in the developing relationship to include the guidance on legislation and CDM 2007 at this stage, although it could be issued after the contract was signed.

4.2 Home works

The architect was somewhat uncomfortable with the client's attitude. The client seemed to resent having to use an architect to get the necessary approvals and was quite certain that he could do everything else including dealing with the party wall issues.

The architect foresaw difficult times ahead and decided that developing the design would prove difficult, so the fee is based on a time charge basis until there was an agreed scheme. However, the architect decided not to assert his moral rights because most of the work was internal improvements.

The customised schedule 'Services for a Small Project' identifies all the services required on the first page, but the second page is included to remind the client what will not be provided.

4.3 A very small commission

This commission for a business client is essentially 'initial design work'. The client has no duties under CDM 2007 at this stage, but the agreement is a 'construction contract'[1] so the requirements of the *Housing Grants, Construction and Regeneration Act 1996* (HGCRA) will apply, e.g. the statutory rights to a withholding notice, suspension and adjudication whether or not specified in the contract. If no specific provisions are made for adjudication, the *Scheme for Construction Contracts Regulations 1998* will apply.

4.4 Inspection and report

This commission (or a survey) is not a 'construction contract' because it does not define the 'construction operations' under HGCRA nor define a 'project' to which CDM 2007 would apply.

---

1 A 'construction contract' means an agreement with a person for the carrying out of construction operations or arranging for the carrying out of construction operations by others or providing his own labour ... and include an agreement to do architectural, design, or surveying work, or to provide advice on building ... in relation to construction operations.

4 Letter Contracts: **Worked examples**

4.1 Worked example: Business works

 **Inigo Wren RIBA Chartered Architect**   2A The Terrace, Barset BS17 7UB

T: 0100 067 089 F: 0100 067 088 E: inigo@wren.com

Mr A Grocer
29 High Street
Barset BS2 8GN

5 September 20XX

My ref: 0XX/022

Dear Mr Grocer

Alterations at 29 High Street Barset.

Thank you for inviting me to act as architect for the alterations and refitting of your shop as described in the attached notes of our meeting on 27th August 20XX.

You told me that your target cost for the building work is £35,000 to which must be added fees and any VAT. You also said that you would like building works to commence on 1st March 20XX.

The services

The services that I am to provide are described in the attached schedule 'Services for a Small Project' in the before-construction and construction stages.

I will also advise you on compliance with statutory legislation and enclose, for your information, a copy of *A client's guide to engaging an architect*, that includes a brief outline of the legislation which may be applicable to this contract and *A client's guide to health and safety for a construction project* that outlines your duties under Construction (Design and Management) Regulations (CDM), which I hope you will find helpful.

It does not appear that it will be necessary to notify your project to the Health and Safety Executive under the CDM Regulations. I confirm giving you on 27th August 20XX an information pack about our competence in relation to these Regulations.

At this time, I do not believe that it will be necessary for you to seek advice from any other consultants. If it becomes necessary to vary the services or to appoint other consultants, I will let you know and we can discuss how to proceed.

I will own the copyright in the drawings and documents that I produce for your project but, subject to payment of fees and/or other amounts properly due, you may copy and use those drawings and documents for purposes related to your project only.

Fees and expenses

My fee in the before-construction period for the preparation, design and construction information stages will be 6% of the pre-tender estimate of the cost of the building work, excluding VAT and fees. For the construction stages my fee will be time based and charged at £70 per hour.

For the measured survey the fee will be a lump sum of £600. Any extra services will be charged at £70 per hour.

In addition to the fees, the cost of copying or purchase of drawings and documents and travel will be charged by the addition of 8% to each account. Other expenses will be charged at net cost. I will ask you to send me a cheque for the fees payable to the local authority before making planning or Building Regulations applications.

I will submit an account for the fees and any expenses or disbursements due each month. Monthly accounts will be based on the estimated percentage of completion. Payment is to be made within 14 days. VAT is not chargeable on my accounts as I am not registered, but if this changes I will let you know.

Please note that if payment of any sums due is not made within 14 days, interest at 8% over the Bank of England base rate, together with the reasonable costs of recovering of the relevant sums, will be payable.

Liability and insurance

My liability to you will expire after six years from completion of the services or, if earlier, practical completion of the construction of the project.

We discussed the events that may give rise to you making a claim against my practice and agreed that a reasonable limit would be £35,000 in respect of each and every claim or series of claims arising out of the same originating cause, within an overall cap of £70,000 for all claims.

I shall maintain, until the expiry of my liability, professional indemnity insurance cover for those amounts. These limits also apply to any claims arising out of the presence of asbestos for any one claim and in the aggregate.

Disputes

I aim to provide a professional standard of service, but if at any time you are not satisfied, please bring the issue to my attention as soon as possible and we can discuss how to resolve the issue. I hope we shall be able to settle the matter by negotiation or mediation. Alternatively, either of us can start court proceedings to settle the dispute at any time.

But nothing shall prevent either of us from referring any dispute to adjudication at any time under the Scheme for Construction Contracts (England and Wales) Regulations 1998. Should we need help in choosing an adjudicator, the nominator will be Royal Institute of British Architects.

You have agreed not to deduct any amount from an account because of an alleged default until the matter is resolved, if necessary by adjudication or in court.

Signing the contract

If you agree with the contents of this letter, please sign both copies of this letter, and initial where indicated both copies of the services schedule and the notes of the meeting on 27th August 20XX, and return one copy of the documents to me. I shall then be in a position to start work.

I am looking forward to working with you on this project.

Yours faithfully

Inigo Wren

Inigo Wren RIBA

Principal: RIBA Membership no: 1234567   ARB Registration no: 987654Z[1]

I confirm that we have read and understood the terms set out in this letter and attachments and that Inigo Wren is to proceed with the services as described.

Signed:_____   Date:_____

for and on behalf of Mr A Grocer

1 Individual architect's are required to be registered with the Architects Registration Board, are subject to its Code and to the disciplinary sanction of the Board in relation to complaints of unacceptable professional conduct or serious professional incompetence.

4.2 Worked example: Home works

Inigo Wren RIBA Chartered Architect
2A The Terrace, Barset BS17 7UB

T: 0100 067 089   F: 0100 067 088   E: inigo@wren.com

Chartered Practice

Mr and Mrs A Homeowner
16 Private Crescent
Thawbridge BS17 5GH

5 September 20XX

My ref: 0XX/024

Dear Mr and Mrs A Homeowner

Alterations at 16 Private Crescent, Thawbridge.

Thank you for inviting me to act as architect for the alterations to your home, which is to be based on the attached sketch proposal developed at our meeting on 1st August 20XX.

You told me that your target cost for the building work is £35,000 to which must be added fees and any VAT. You also said that you would like building works to commence on 1st March 20XX.

The services

My services are described in the attached schedule 'Services for a Small Project' in the before-construction stages. You told me that you will manage the construction stages including obtaining tenders and overseeing the building work.

When the extent of any work affecting the common wall with the adjoining property is determined, we can discuss the application of the Party Wall Act. Please note that it may be necessary to appoint a party wall surveyor if your neighbour objects to the work.

At this time, I do not believe it will be necessary for you to seek advice from any other consultants. If it becomes necessary to vary the services or to appoint other consultants, I will let you know and we can discuss how to proceed.

I own the copyright in the drawings and documents that I produce for your project, but subject to payment of my accounts, you may copy and use those drawings and documents for purposes related to your project only.

Fees and expenses

My fee for the services outlined in the services schedule will be
- £70 per hour for stages AB and CD;
- a lump sum of £500 for stages EFG construction information;
- a lump sum of £600 for the measured survey of your property.

Any other services will be charged at £70 per hour.

My fee includes my expenses for the copying or purchase of drawings and documents or travel. Other expenses will be charged at net cost. I will ask you to send me a cheque for the fees payable to the local authority before making planning or Building Regulations applications.

I will submit an account for the fees and any expenses or disbursements due each month based on the estimated percentage of completion. Payment is to be made within 14 days. VAT is not chargeable on my accounts as I am not registered, but if this changes I will let you know.

Please note that if payment of any sums due is not made within 14 days, simple interest at 8% over the Bank of England base, rate together with reasonable debt recovery costs, will be payable.

Liability and insurance

We discussed the events that may give rise to you making a claim against my practice and agreed that a reasonable limit would be £35,000 in respect of each and every claim or series of claims arising out of the same originating cause with an overall cap on all claims of £75,000.

My liability to you for loss or damage will be limited to that amount. Any such liability will expire after six years from completion of the services.

Disputes

I aim to provide a professional standard of service, but if at any time you are not satisfied, please bring the issue to my attention as soon as possible and we can discuss how to resolve the issue.

Signing the contract

If you agree with the contents of this letter, please sign both copies of this letter, and initial, where indicated, both copies of the services schedule and the sketch proposal and return one copy of the documents to me. I shall then be in a position to start work.

I enclose, for your information, a copy of *Working with an architect for your home* which I hope you will find helpful.

I am looking forward to working with you on this project.

Yours faithfully

Inigo Wren

Inigo Wren RIBA[1]

Principal: RIBA Membership no: 1234567   ARB Registration no: 987654Z

I confirm that we have read and understood the terms set out in this letter and attachments and that Inigo Wren is to proceed with the services as described.

Signed: _____   Date: _____

for and on behalf of Mr and Mrs Homeowner

---

[1] Individual architects are required to be registered with the Architects Registration Board, are subject to its Code and to the disciplinary sanction of the Board in relation to complaints of unacceptable professional conduct or serious professional incompetence.

4.2 Worked example: Schedule 'Services for a small project'

Inigo Wren RIBA Chartered Architect
2A The Terrace, Barset BS17 7UB

T: 0100 067 089 F: 0100 067 088 E: inigo@wren.com

RIBA Chartered Practice

The services are performed in accordance with this schedule in stages: **AB, CD** and **EF**

Before construction

AB: Preparation

Y	Visit the property and carry out an initial appraisal
Y	Assist the client in preparing the client's requirements
n/a	Identify alternative solutions for the project
Y	Advise on the need for services by consultants or specialists
LS	Survey and prepare drawings of site and/or buildings as required
Y	Arrange investigation of soil or structural conditions

CD: Design

Y	Prepare a preliminary design and discuss with the client
Y	Develop the final design
Y	Prepare an approximate estimate of cost
Y	Submit the final design proposals and approximate cost for approval
Y	Provide services in connection with party wall negotiations
Y	Make an application for detailed planning permission

EFG: Construction information

n/a	Coordinate and integrate any designs provided by others
Y	Prepare drawings and other information in sufficient detail to enable a tender or tenders to be obtained
Y	Prepare drawings and other information required for construction
Y	Make an application for Building Regulations approval
a	Prepare (a) a specification (b) schedule of works
Y	Advise on an appropriate form of building contract, its conditions and the responsibilities of the client, the architect and the builder

---

This is the schedule 'Services for a Small Project' referred to in the agreement relating to the project: *Alterations to 16 Private Crescent, Thawbridge*

Between *Mr and Mrs Homeowner* _____ and Inigo Wren RIBA _____
                              Initials   *Initials*

Construction

H: Tender action
- [n/a] Prepare documents required for tendering purposes
- [n/a] Advise on builders to be invited to tender for the work
- [n/a] Invite, appraise and report on tenders
- [n/a]

JK: Construction work
- [n/a] Advise on the appointment of a builder
- [n/a] Prepare the building contract and arrange for it to be signed
- [n/a] Provide the builder with the information required for construction
- [n/a] Visit the site to see that the work is proceeding generally in accordance with the contract
- [n/a] Certify payments for work carried out or completed; advise on final cost
- [n/a] Provide or obtain record drawings showing the building and its services
- [n/a] Give general advice on maintenance
- [n/a]

L: After handover
- [n/a] Make final inspections and arrange for correction of any defects
- [n/a] Agree final account and issue a final certificate
- [n/a]

Other services
- [n/a]
- [n/a]
- [n/a]
- [n/a]
- [n/a]

The following activities do not form part of the services unless identified as 'Other services' above:
- Models and special drawings
- Negotiating approvals by statutory authorities
- Making submissions to and negotiating approvals by landlords, freeholders, etc
- Preparing a schedule of dilapidations
- Services in connection with party wall negotiations
- Negotiating a price with a builder (in lieu of tendering)
- Dealing with extensions of time, and contractor's claims
- Services in any dispute between the client and another party
- Services following damage by fire and other causes
- Services following suspension, termination of any contract or agreement with, or the insolvency of, any other party providing services to the project
- Services in connection with government and other grants

4.3 Worked example: A very small commission

Inigo Wren RIBA Chartered Architect   **2A The Terrace, Barset BS17 7UB**

T: 0100 067 089   F: 0100 067 088   E: inigo@nwren.com

Toymakers Ltd   5 September 20XX
2 The Green
Barset BS3 6QG   My ref: 0XX/023

For the attention of Mr E Blyton

Dear Sir

Crèche at 2 The Green Barset

Thank you for inviting me to make a survey of the canteen block and apply for outline planning permission for alterations and an extension to the building to provide crèche facilities for staff.

At this time I do not believe that it will be necessary for you to seek advice from any other consultants.

I am enclosing a copy of *A client's guide to engaging an architect*, which I hope you will find helpful. At this stage, you have no duties under the CDM Regulations 2007. If outline planning permission is granted, we can discuss how these matters will affect the development of the design and the building work.

My fee for the survey will be a lump sum of £600. My fee for preparing the information and making the outline planning application will be charged at £70 per hour, for which I suggest you should allow a budget of £1,500. My fees include my expenses. However, I will ask you to send me a cheque for the fees payable to the local authority before making the planning application.

I will submit two accounts, the first on completion of the survey and the second before making the planning application. Payment is to be made within 14 days. VAT is not chargeable on my accounts as I am not registered, but if this changes I will let you know.

I own the copyright in the drawings and documents that I produce for your project. You may copy and use those drawings and documents for purposes related to your project only, subject to payment of fees and/or other amounts properly due. Your right to copy and use does not extend to any future purchaser, leaseholder or tenant of your property without my prior agreement.

My liability to you in respect of each and every claim or series of claims arising out of the same originating cause on this commission is limited to £10,000, which we agreed is a reasonable sum to cover the risks. Any such liability will expire after six years from completion of the services.

I aim to provide a professional standard of service, but if at any time you are not satisfied, or if you believe that you have a claim against my practice, please bring the issue to my attention as soon as possible and we can discuss how to resolve the issue.

If you agree that this is a correct record of our discussions, please sign both copies of this letter and return one copy to me. I shall then be in a position to start work.

I am looking forward to working with you on this project.

Yours faithfully

Inigo Wren

Inigo Wren RIBA[1]

Principal: RIBA Membership no: 1234567　　　　　ARB Registration no: 987654Z

I confirm that we have read and understood the terms set out in this letter and attachments and that Inigo Wren is to proceed with the services as described.

Signed: _____　　　Date: _____

for and on behalf of Toymakers Ltd

---

[1] Individual architects are required to be registered with the Architects Registration Board, are subject to its Code and to the disciplinary sanction of the Board in relation to complaints of unacceptable professional conduct or serious professional incompetence.

4.4 Worked example: Inspection and report

Toymakers Ltd
2 The Green
Barset BS3 6QG

5 September 20XX

My ref: 0XX/014

Inigo Wren RIBA
Chartered Architect

For the attention of Mr E Blyton

Dear Sir

Inspection and report on 3 The Green Barset

Thank you for inviting me to make a visual inspection of your property and to report on its suitability for change of use to the offices. My report will take into account our discussion as recorded in the attached notes of our meeting on 29th August 20XX. Please let me know if you have any comments on the notes.

My fee for the inspection and report will be £600.00 plus VAT. My fee includes my expenses.

I will own the copyright in the report but, subject to payment of fees and/or other amounts properly due, you may copy the report for marketing or negotiations with potential purchasers, leaseholders or tenants of your property.

My liability to you or to any future purchaser, leaseholder or tenant of your property in respect of each and every claim or series of claims arising out of the same originating cause on this commission is limited to £10,000. Any such liability will expire after six years from completion of the services.

If you agree that this is a correct record of our discussions, please sign both copies of this letter, initial the attached notes and return one copy of each document to me. I shall then be in a position to start work.

Yours faithfully

Inigo Wren

Inigo Wren RIBA[1]

I confirm that I have read and understood the terms set out in this letter and that Inigo Wren is to proceed with the services described.

Domestic Architecture
Barn Conversions
Interior Design
Exhibitions
Conservation
Industrial
Offices
Retail

2A The Terrace
Barset BS17 7UB
T: 0100 067 089
F: 0100 067 088
E: inigo@wren.com

Signed: _____ Date: _____
for and on behalf of Toymakers Ltd

---

[1] Individual architects are required to be registered with the Architects Registration Board, are subject to its Code and to the disciplinary sanction of the Board in relation to complaints of unacceptable professional conduct or serious professional incompetence.

Further reading

Lupton, S., *Architect's Handbook of Practice Management,* 7th edition, RIBA Enterprises (London, 2001).

Phillips, R., *Good Practice Guide: Fee Management,* RIBA Publishing (London, forthcoming 2009).

Phillips, R., *Guide to RIBA Agreements 2009,* RIBA Publishing, (London, forthcoming 2009).

RIBA, *A client's guide to engaging an architect,* RIBA Publishing (London, 2009).

RIBA, *A client's guide to health and safety for a construction project,* RIBA Publishing (London, 2007).

RIBA, *RIBA Code of Professional Conduct,* RIBA (London, 2005).

RIBA, *Working with an architect for your home,* available to download free of charge at www.architecture.com/useanarchitect.

RIBA Agreements 2007

RIBA, *Concise Agreement for the appointment of an Architect* (C-Con-07-A), RIBA Publishing, (London, 2007).
Available to purchase in print or online at www.ribabookshops.com/agreements.
To be replaced by the forthcoming *Concise Agreement.*

RIBA, *Domestic Project Agreement for the appointment of an Architect* (D-Con-07-A), RIBA Publishing (London, 2007).
Available to purchase in print or online www.ribabookshops.com/agreements.
To be replaced by the forthcoming *Domestic Project Agreement.*